Atlanta
DREAM

by Charlie Beattie

Copyright © 2026 by Press Room Editions. All rights reserved. No part of this book may be used or reproduced in any manner whatsoever, including internet usage, without written permission from the copyright owner, except in the case of brief quotations embodied in critical articles and reviews.

Book design by Kate Liestman
Cover design by Kate Liestman

Photographs ©: Darron Cummings/AP Images, cover; Alex Slitz/Getty Images Sport/Getty Images, 4; Mitchell Leff/Getty Images Sport/Getty Images, 7, 27, 29; Ronald Martinez/Getty Images Sport/Getty Images, 8; Jessica Hill/AP Images, 10; Danny Moloshok/AP Images, 13; Paul Beaty/AP Images, 15; Nick Wass/AP Images, 16; Erik S. Lesser/AP Images, 19; Hannah Foslien/Getty Images Sport/Getty Images, 21; Leon Bennett/Getty Images Sport/Getty Images, 23, 24

Press Box Books, an imprint of Press Room Editions.

ISBN
979-8-89469-009-4 (library bound)
979-8-89469-022-3 (paperback)
979-8-89469-047-6 (epub)
979-8-89469-035-3 (hosted ebook)

Library of Congress Control Number: 2025930748

Distributed by North Star Editions, Inc.
2297 Waters Drive
Mendota Heights, MN 55120
www.northstareditions.com

Printed in the United States of America
082025

ABOUT THE AUTHOR

Charlie Beattie is a writer, editor, and former sportscaster. Originally from Saint Paul, Minnesota, he now lives in Charleston, South Carolina, with his wife and son.

TABLE of CONTENTS

CHAPTER 1
HOWARD GOES OFF   5

CHAPTER 2
BEGINNING OF A DREAM 11

CHAPTER 3
BEASTS OF THE EAST   17

SUPERSTAR PROFILE
ANGEL McCOUGHTRY   22

CHAPTER 4
A DREAM RETURN   25

QUICK STATS   30
GLOSSARY   31
TO LEARN MORE   32
INDEX   32

CHAPTER 1

HOWARD GOES OFF

Rhyne Howard scanned the floor. The 6-foot-2 (188-cm) guard took two dribbles to create space from her defender. Then she drifted back behind the three-point line and shot. The ball swished through the net.

Howard and the Atlanta Dream were playing the Los Angeles Sparks during the 2023 season. Howard's

Rhyne Howard averaged 17.5 points per game during the 2023 season.

three-pointer put the Dream up 71–61 midway through the third quarter. Fans filled every seat in Atlanta's arena. Dream fans couldn't get enough of watching Howard.

Atlanta had selected Howard in the 2022 Women's National Basketball Association (WNBA) Draft. At the time, the Dream badly needed scoring. So, Atlanta took Howard with the top pick. The University of Kentucky star was exactly what the Dream needed. Howard had led her conference in scoring twice at Kentucky. She then provided offense right away for Atlanta. In 2022, she won the WNBA Rookie of the Year Award.

Howard made 35 percent of her three-pointers in 2023.

Now in her second year, Howard was having a career day against the Sparks. She scored 17 points in the first quarter. By halftime, she had 25. Howard's three-pointer in the third quarter tied her career high of 33.

Howard made the WNBA All-Star Game in her first two seasons with the Dream.

Late in the third quarter, Dream guard Haley Jones had the ball. Howard stood under the basket. With a quick move, Howard shook her defender. Jones fired a pass. Howard leaped to grab it. In one motion, she banked the ball off the backboard. The alley-oop gave Howard 35 points on the night.

Howard continued scoring from there. She finished the game with 43 points. That total was one point shy of the Atlanta record for points in a game. And Howard didn't stop there. In 2023, she led the Dream back to the playoffs for the first time in five years.

THREE-POINT EXPERT

Howard drained six three-pointers against the Sparks. During the 2023 season, she made a three-pointer in 38 of the 39 games she played. Howard also sank her 100th three-pointer in just 40 career games. No player in WNBA history had reached that mark faster.

CHAPTER 2

BEGINNING OF A DREAM

In October 2007, the WNBA held a press conference. It took place in Atlanta's Centennial Olympic Park. The city had hosted the Olympics in 1996. Women's basketball was a popular event at those Games. The WNBA started a year later. Then, in 2007, the league announced that a new team would play in Atlanta.

Betty Lennox (22) made 42 percent of her shots in 2008, her only season with Atlanta.

By January 2008, the new team had a name. Fans voted for "Dream" in an online contest. Two months later, head coach and general manager Marynell Meadors put together the team. The league held an expansion draft. Meadors picked one player from each of the other 13 teams.

Betty Lennox turned into the team's first star. The 5-foot-8 (173-cm) guard could light it up from deep. She led the Dream by

ATLANTA'S FIRST PROS

The WNBA started in 1997. At the time, Atlanta had a professional women's basketball team. But the Atlanta Glory played in a different league. They were in the American Basketball League (ABL). However, the Glory folded in March 1998. It took more than a decade for a women's basketball team to return to Atlanta.

Ivory Latta averaged 11.4 points per game in 2008.

averaging 17.5 points per game in the 2008 season. On June 27, the Dream faced the Connecticut Sun. Lennox came out firing. She hit 17 of her 32 shots. Five of those buckets were three-pointers.

The game went into overtime. Lennox finished with 44 points. She became just the sixth player to score 40 or more points in a WNBA game. However, the Dream lost to the Sun 109–101.

That game continued a rough streak for Atlanta. The team lost its first 17 games. No WNBA team had ever had such a bad start to a season. The losing streak finally ended on July 5. That night, six players scored at least 10 points for the Dream. Guard Ivory Latta and forward Jennifer Lacy led the way with 18 points each. Atlanta beat the Chicago Sky 91–84.

The Dream finished the year 4–30. Atlanta had the worst record in the league. But better days were ahead.

Jennifer Lacy scored a season-high 18 points two different times in 2008.

CHAPTER 3

BEASTS OF THE EAST

The Dream drafted Angel McCoughtry with the top pick in 2009. That season, the 6-foot-1 (185-cm) forward earned WNBA Rookie of the Year honors. In 2010, she led the Dream in scoring. Then she shined in the playoffs. She scored 49 points in the first round. Atlanta swept the Washington Mystics in two games.

Angel McCoughtry (center) averaged more than 20 points per game in five different seasons with the Dream.

In the next round, Atlanta faced the New York Liberty. McCoughtry scored 21 points in Game 1. In Game 2, McCoughtry couldn't miss. New York had no answer for her. She piled up 42 points. That set a WNBA playoff record. Atlanta won 105–93 to clinch a spot in the Finals.

Atlanta faced the Seattle Storm in the Finals. In Game 1, the Dream lost by only two points. Then the Dream lost by three in Game 2.

HONORING AN ICON

The team name "Dream" comes from one of America's most inspiring moments. On August 28, 1963, Atlanta native Martin Luther King Jr. gave his famous "I Have a Dream" speech in Washington, DC. The speech was a key moment in the Civil Rights Movement.

Dream players celebrate clinching their spot in the 2010 WNBA Finals.

And in Game 3, the Storm completed the sweep with another three-point win.

Those close calls left the Dream hungry to get back. They didn't have to wait too long. In 2011, McCoughtry led the way again. She scored the most points

19

in the WNBA that year. McCoughtry carried Atlanta back to the Finals. But the Minnesota Lynx swept the Dream to win the title.

In 2013, the Dream finished with a 17–17 record. Then they lost their playoff opener to the Washington Mystics. One more loss would end their season. However, the team caught fire after that. McCoughtry and guard Tiffany Hayes handled the scoring. Inside, forward Erika de Souza grabbed lots of rebounds. Atlanta won four straight games to return to the Finals.

Once again, the Dream faced the Minnesota Lynx. Minnesota had been the WNBA's best team all year. That strength

Tiffany Hayes averaged 13.8 points per game over her 10 seasons with Atlanta.

showed in the Finals. The Lynx shut down McCoughtry. Minnesota won in another sweep.

SUPERSTAR PROFILE

ANGEL McCOUGHTRY

The Dream struggled in their first season. But they got a big reward with the top pick in the 2009 draft. Forward Angel McCoughtry had been a star at the University of Louisville. She proved to be just what Atlanta needed.

For 10 seasons, McCoughtry was the team's go-to scorer. She won the WNBA scoring title twice. And she always played at her best in the playoffs. In 2010, McCoughtry averaged 26.7 points per game in the playoffs. A year later, she averaged 31 points per game in the Finals.

McCoughtry could score from inside and outside. Many of her best highlights came on hard drives to the basket. She was a creative passer. And she played strong defense. When McCoughtry left the team in 2020, she held many team records. She led Atlanta in points, assists, and steals.

McCoughtry averaged 22.8 points per game in the playoffs during her time with Atlanta.

CHAPTER 4

A DREAM RETURN

On July 11, 2018, the Dream beat the Washington Mystics 106–89. Guards Tiffany Hayes and Renee Montgomery both scored more than 20 points. So did forwards Angel McCoughtry and Jessica Breland. Four teammates scoring 20 points each in a game had happened only once before in WNBA history.

Renee Montgomery played the final two seasons of her 11-year career with Atlanta

At 23–11, Atlanta boasted its best record ever. The Dream finished first in the East. But by the playoffs, they had a huge problem. McCoughtry suffered a knee injury late in the year. Without her, Atlanta fell to Washington in the playoffs.

McCoughtry never played for Atlanta again. The Dream dropped in the standings. The team needed a fresh start.

PLAYING FOR CHANGE

In 2020, the WNBA supported the Black Lives Matter movement. Atlanta owner Kelly Loeffler criticized her players for doing so. Loeffler was a United States senator from Georgia at the time. Dream players demanded that she sell the team. They also campaigned for her opponent, Raphael Warnock. He won the election in January 2021. Loeffler sold the team a month later.

After joining the Dream in 2023, Allisha Gray (15) made the All-Star Game in her first two seasons with Atlanta.

Atlanta began by changing its uniforms. The team also switched home arenas. Tanisha Wright took over as the team's new coach before the 2022 season.

In 2023, Atlanta battled for a playoff spot all season. The team featured many talented players. Forward

Rhyne Howard earned All-Star honors. Veteran guard Allisha Gray averaged more than 17 points per game. Inside, forward Cheyenne Parker led the team in rebounding.

With three games left in the season, Atlanta hosted the Seattle Storm. A win would send the Dream back to the playoffs. Gray and Howard both struggled to make shots. But Atlanta received a boost. Monique Billings had come off the bench for most of the season. The forward finished with 15 points and 14 rebounds. Billings lifted the Dream to a 79–68 win.

The Dallas Wings swept the Dream in the first round. The quick playoff

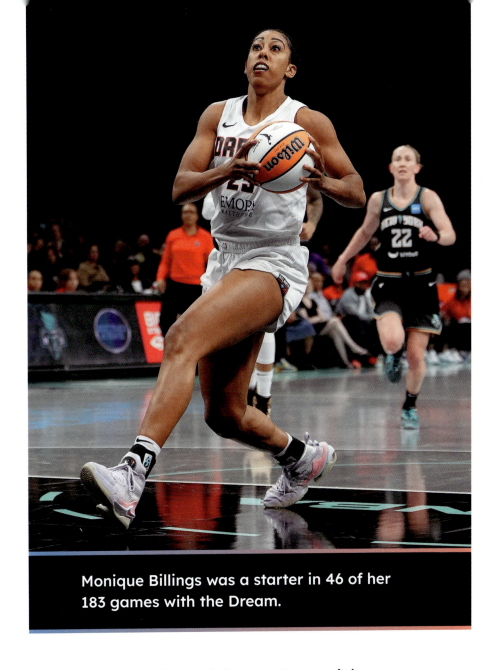

Monique Billings was a starter in 46 of her 183 games with the Dream.

exit disappointed fans. But with young stars on the team, Atlanta hoped a championship was just around the corner.

QUICK STATS

ATLANTA DREAM

Founded: 2008

Championships: 0

Key coaches:

- Marynell Meadors (2008-12): 73-87, 8-9 playoffs
- Fred Williams (2012-13): 24-20, 5-6 playoffs
- Nicki Collen (2018-20): 38-52, 2-3 playoffs

Most career points: Angel McCoughtry (5,468)

Most career assists: Angel McCoughtry (860)

Most career rebounds: Sancho Lyttle (1,877)

Most career steals: Angel McCoughtry (597)

Most career blocks: Elizabeth Williams (331)

Stats are accurate through the 2024 season.

GLOSSARY

alley-oop
When a player catches a pass while in the air and shoots the ball before landing.

assists
Passes that lead directly to a teammate scoring a basket.

draft
An event that allows teams to choose new players coming into the league.

expansion draft
A special draft that allows a new team to select players from existing teams.

general manager
The person in a team's front office who drafts and signs new players.

press conference
An event held to make an announcement to the media.

rookie
A first-year player.

veteran
A player who has spent several years in a league.

TO LEARN MORE

Graves, Will. *Basketball*. Abdo Publishing, 2024.

O'Neal, Ciara. *The WNBA Finals*. Apex Editions, 2023.

Wagner, Zelda. *Basketball Superstars*. Lerner Publications, 2025.

MORE INFORMATION

To learn more about the Atlanta Dream go to **pressboxbooks.com/AllAccess**. These links are routinely monitored and updated to provide the most current information available.

INDEX

Atlanta Glory, 12

Billings, Monique, 28
Breland, Jessica, 25

Connecticut Sun, 13–14

de Souza, Erika, 20

Gray, Allisha, 28

Hayes, Tiffany, 20, 25
Howard, Rhyne, 5–9, 28

Jones, Haley, 8

King, Martin Luther, Jr., 18

Lacy, Jennifer, 14
Latta, Ivory, 14
Lennox, Betty, 12–14
Loeffler, Kelly, 26
Los Angeles Sparks, 5, 7, 9

McCoughtry, Angel, 17–21, 22, 25–26
Meadors, Marynell, 12
Minnesota Lynx, 20–21
Montgomery, Renee, 25

New York Liberty, 18

Parker, Cheyenne, 28

Seattle Storm, 18–19, 28

Warnock, Raphael, 26
Washington Mystics, 17, 20, 25–26
Wright, Tanisha, 27